ROME
a day

Scenes from the Eternal City

The Paper Mermaid Press

For my parents, Peter and Cynthia Rockwell,
who gave me this city, and so much more.
~ M. F.

To Phineas, Zane, and Frances, who will
spend many days in Rome, I hope.
~ S. D. K.

Pictures © by Mary Faino
Words © by S. D. Kelly
All Rights Reserved

ISBN   978-1-7322085-0-6
First Edition, May 2018
Published by **The Paper Mermaid, LLC**
57 Main Street, Rockport, MA 01966

www.papermermaid.com

ROME a day

Pictures by
Mary Faino

Words by
S. D. Kelly

Pull aside the curtain to see Rome,
see the stars above St. Peter's,
in the quiet hours before morning,
before the city fills with light.

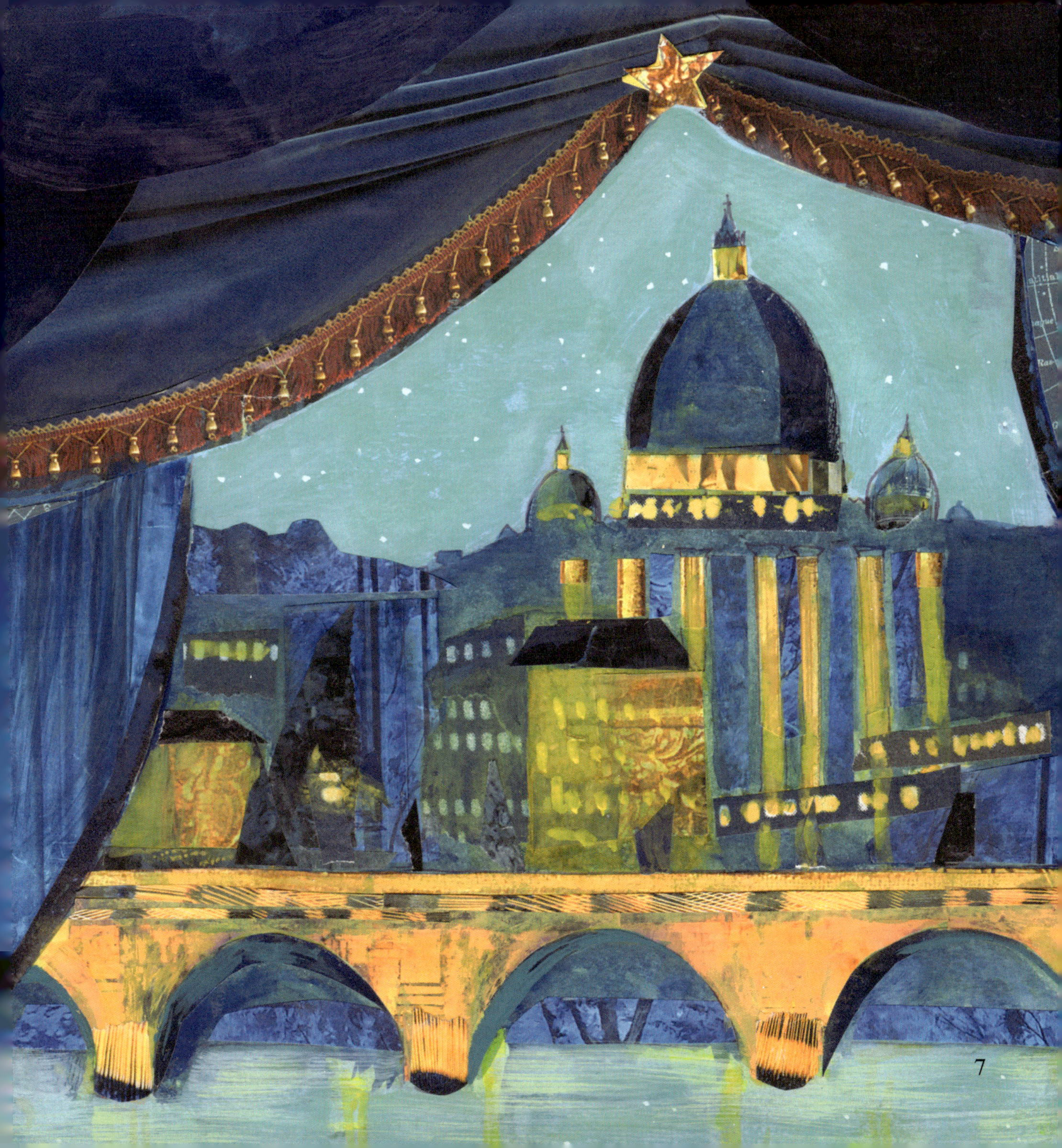

The cats come to the Forum
to stalk and to sleep.
Soon all the people will arrive
to walk the old, old roads.

But not yet. It is still too early.
Just before the sun comes up.

North
Pole
Lynx
Cancer
The Clock
The Net
Ship Argo
Corona
Borealis
Bootes
Great Bear

The glow of the morning light
rounds the Colosseum.
Steps go up, up
to the top, up to the sky.

We remember the glory of Rome!
Here, in the beams of the rising sun.

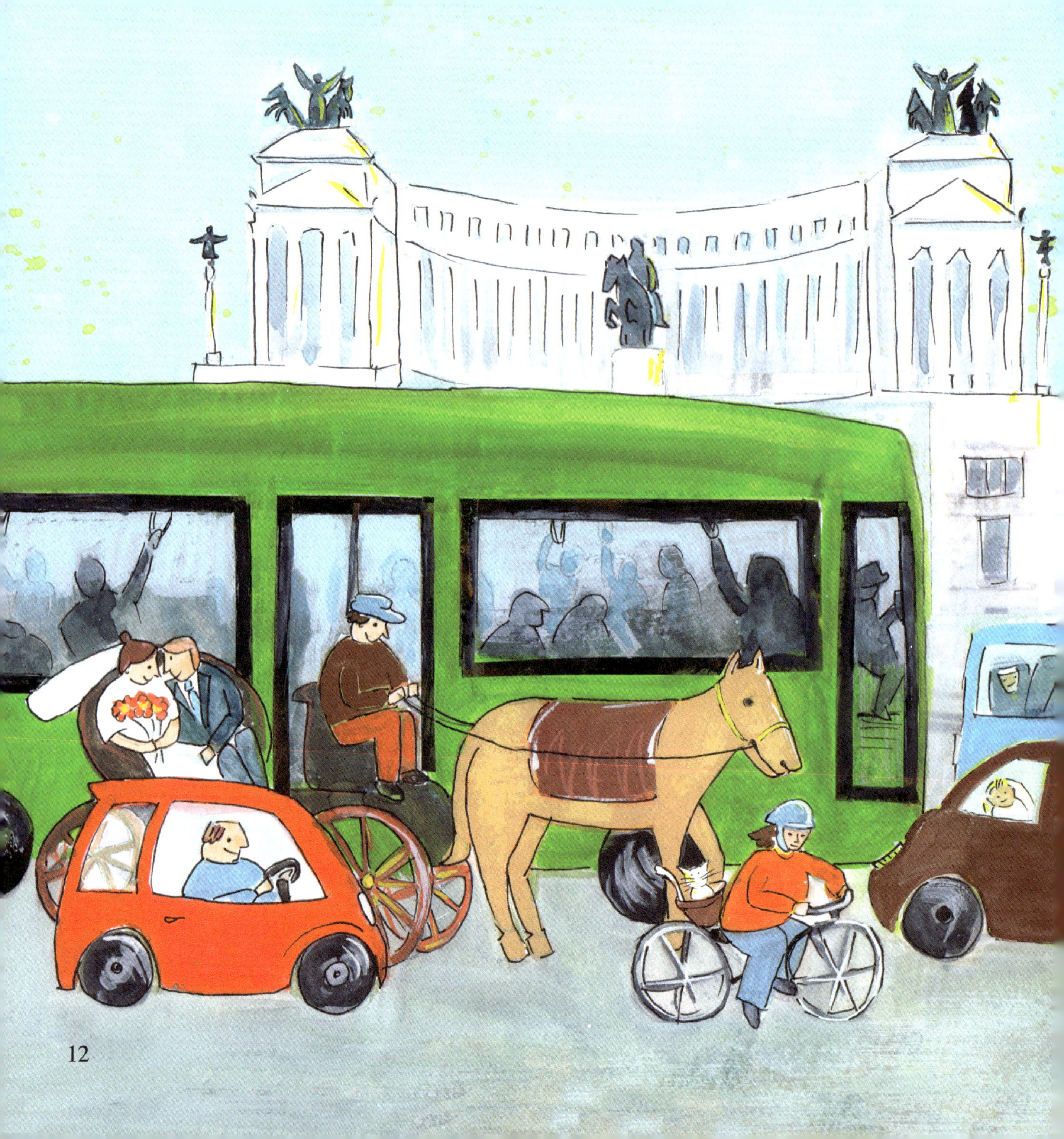

White, white marble
far above the piazza.
All of Rome moves through the square.

La vigile directs, gloves
flashing in the brightness
of the early morning sun.

Buy the flowers, *compra i fiori*
(and don't forget the olives!)
before they are cleared away.

Friar Bruno stands in his cloak,
unmovable, still,
in the heat of the late morning sun.

15

The Petals fall once a year at Pentecost. The Pantheon echoes with the sound of footsteps. It echoed then and echoes now.

Look up! To see the dome, open to the light of the midday sun.

Stop for food along the way,
here and there and here again.
The pizza is fresh and hot.

Let's eat outside,
mangiamo al fresco
shaded from the rays of the noonday sun.

19

20

A stroll in the park after lunch:
Pulcinella is silly. He says hello,
while Garibaldi's men look on.
Viva Roma! Viva L'Italia!

The soldiers watch over Rome
from the top of the hill,
standing upright in the afternoon sun.

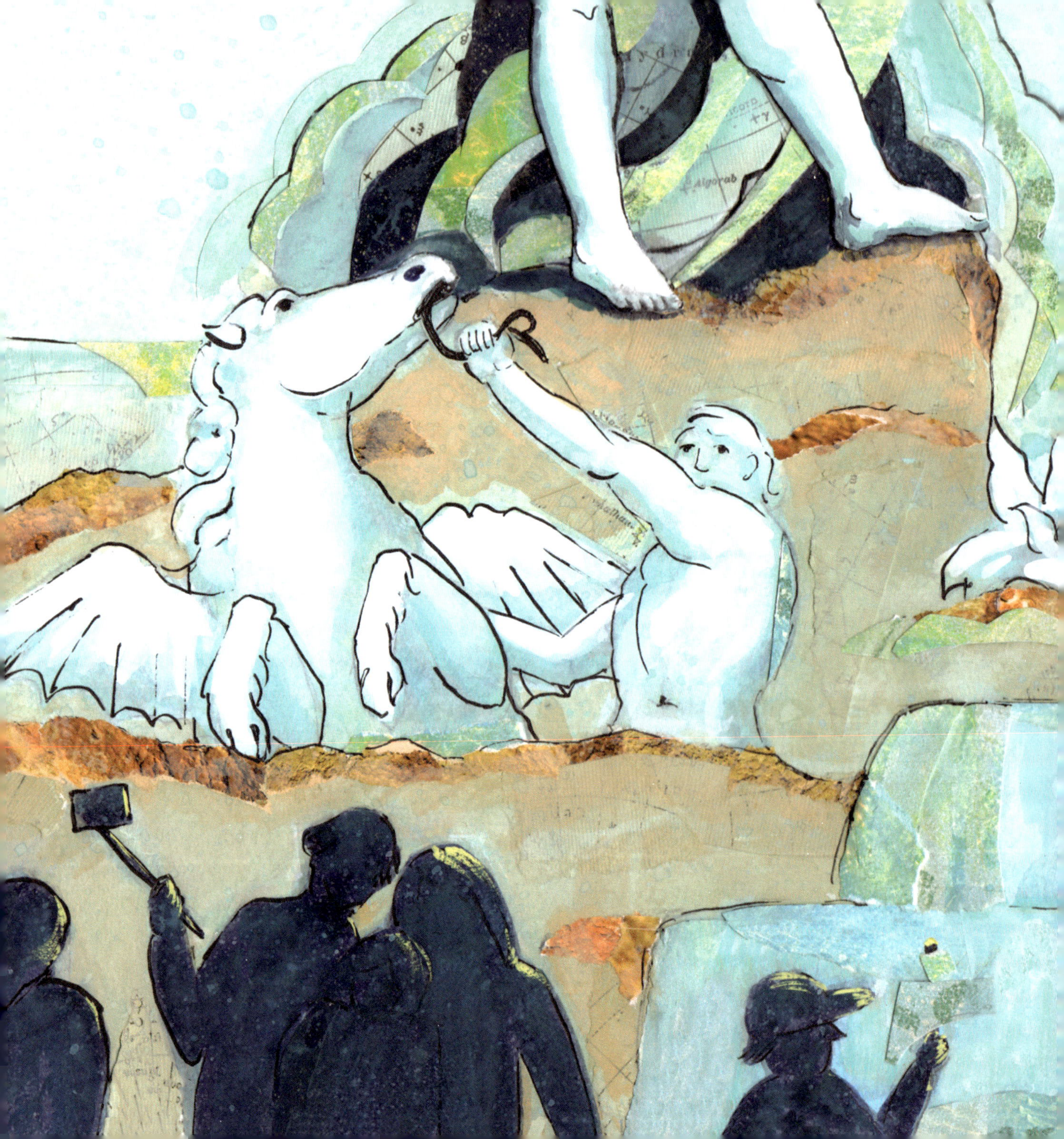

The fountain crowds the square
and the people crowd the fountain,
coins and cameras in hand.
Take your turn and toss a coin.

Now you will come back to see the tritons,
all the creatures of myth,
tumbling forever
in the glow of the sun.

The Tiber moves through the heart of Rome.
Once a mighty river, now it is quiet,
hemmed in by walls.

Take a walk along the water,
below the domes and bridges
below the light of the fading sun.

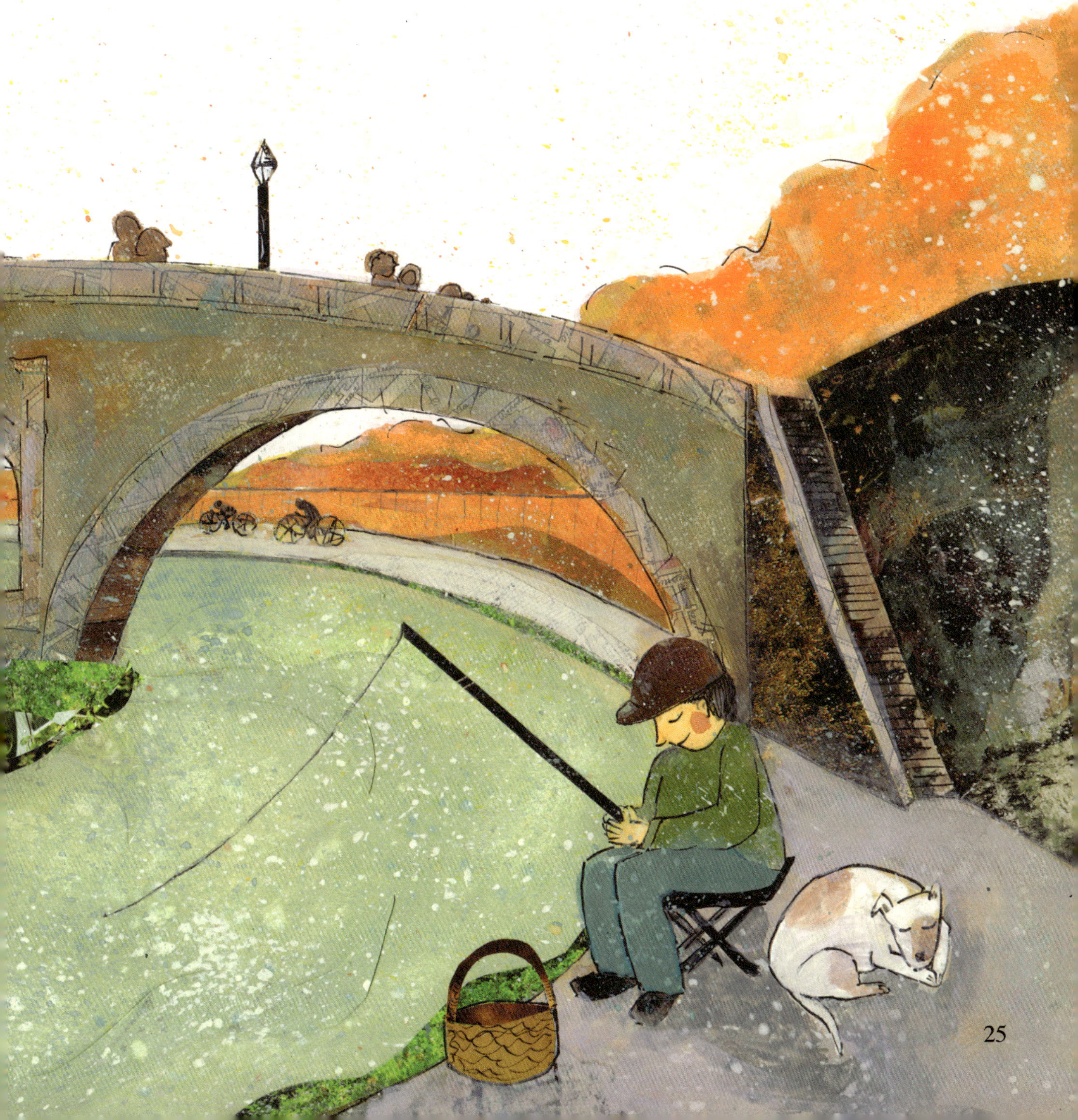

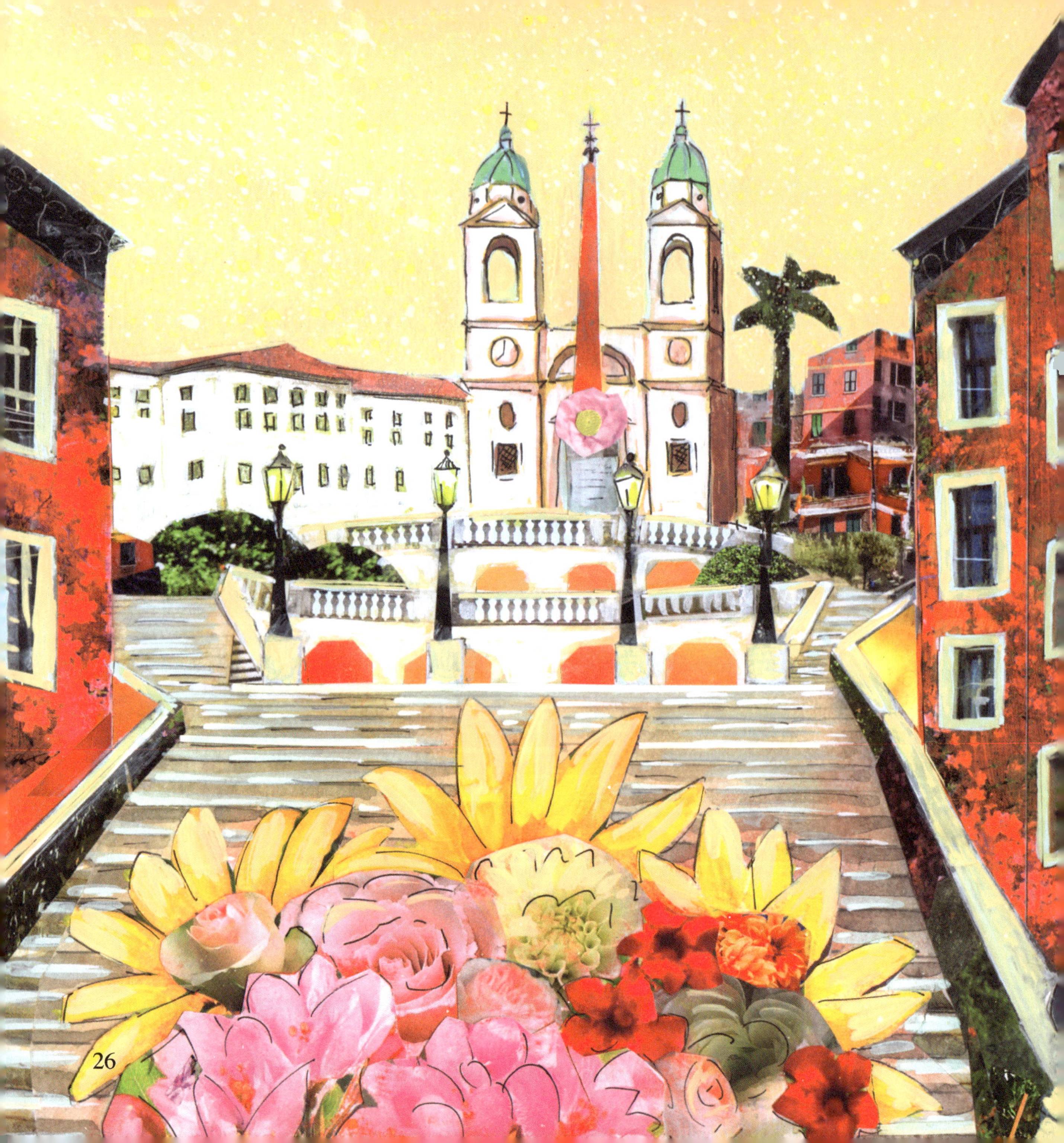

Climb, climb to the top of the steps.
past the travelers who eternally love Rome,
past the painters and the poets
(who have never ceased to be).

Sit down and take a rest,
sit down in the warmth of the late day sun.

Look out over the city, out over the lights.
See the swallows as they swoop, higher even than all the basilicas of Rome.

Listen to the music of the evening sun.

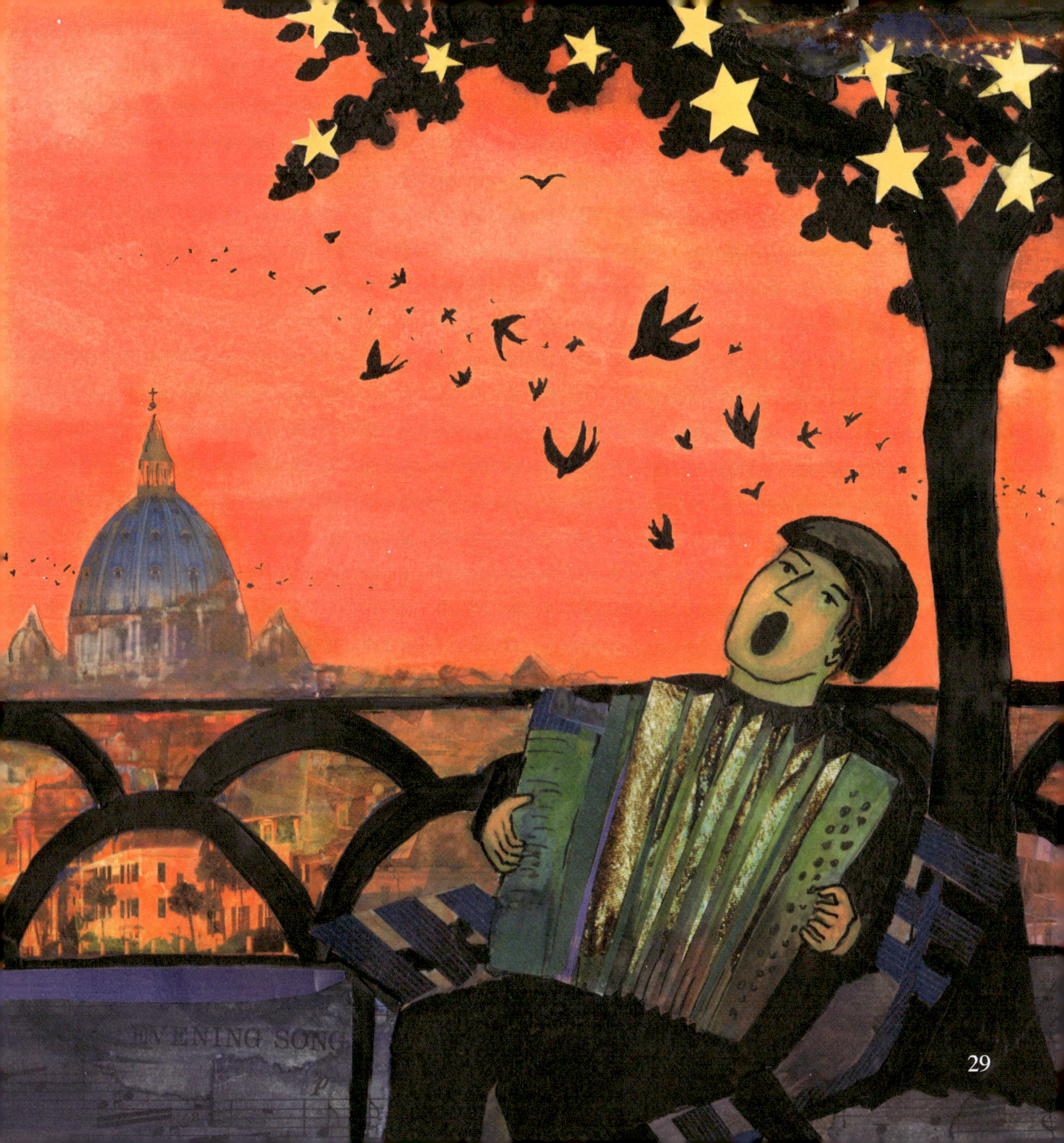
EVENING SONG

Go to sleep and dre[am]

The tired cat leaps up to sleep
on a cradle of stone.
The curtain closes
on the settling dark.

The time has come to say goodnight.
Buona notte, Roma.
Goodnight, goodnight
Rome.

Rome is an old city. It was founded 28 centuries ago, in 753 B.C., though the site of Rome has been occupied even longer. After its founding, Rome grew in power, with rulers who took over much of the known world. By the 1st century B.C., the poet Tibullus called Rome "the eternal city". Rome seemed like a place that would go on and on, a city without an end. It was impossible to imagine the world without Rome. It turns out that Tibullus was right: two thousand years later, it still seems impossible, and we still call Rome the eternal city.

The Places in **ROME a day:**

St. Peter's Basilica (p. 7) is both a tomb and a church, the place where tradition holds that St. Peter himself is buried, along with many other popes from the Catholic Church. The present-day pope holds church services at the basilica and in the square outside. Thousands of pilgrims from all over the world come to visit St. Peter's.

The **Forum (pp. 8-9)** is the heart of ancient Rome. It is the old city square and market place, where everyone gathered to buy food and argue politics and celebrate military victories. Now it is a ruin, but we can still walk the same roads the ancient Romans walked. The feral cats of Rome are famous, and often live among the ruins. The ladies that feed them are known as *gattare* (*gatto* means cat in Italian).

When the **Colosseum (pp. 10-11)** was built nearly 2,000 years ago, the emperor Titus celebrated by hosting over 100 days of games there. It was a fun party, designed to show off one of the biggest amphitheatres ever built – one that could hold up to 80,000 people! The Colosseum was also called the *Vomitorium*, because it was able to quickly vomit, or spew out, all the thousands of people who were inside, thanks to the design of the building with its many doorways and exits.

Piazza Venezia **(pp. 12-13)** serves as the modern hub of Rome, where several main roads intersect. It is a very busy place. The giant building overlooking the *piazza* is named L'Altare della Patria, but has a few nicknames too, one of which is "The Wedding Cake". *L'Altare della Patria* is now a monument to the fallen soldier, but was originally built to honor the first king of a unified Italy, Victor Emmanuel II in the 19th century.

A statue of Giordano Bruno stands in the ***Campo di Fiori*** **(pp. 14-15)** or Field of Flowers, one of the most famous markets in Rome. Bruno was burned at the stake for heresy in 1600, right in the square. Every year on the anniversary of his death, philosophers and freethinkers gather to place a wreath at his statue.

The **Pantheon (pp. 16-17)** was rebuilt all the way back in 126 A.D, but unlike other ancient buildings, the *Pantheon* is not a ruin. It is still in use – these days as a church. The oculus, a window at the very top of the *Pantheon*, is open to the sky and weather. At the annual religious celebration of Pentecost, a shower of rose petals is released through the oculus, with the petals drifting down onto the crowds of people below.

Visiting **Trastevere (pp. 18-19)** is one of the highlights of Rome. With its winding, cobblestoned streets, small restaurants, picturesque buildings, and cozy shops – many of which are run by artisans – *Trastevere* features some of the best aspects of day-to-day life in Rome.

The **Gianicolo (pp. 20-21)** is known as the 8th hill of Rome (it is not one of the seven hills of Rome since it is outside the city walls). The *Gianicolo* overlooks the city and contains all sorts of interesting things, including a puppet show, and a statue of Giuseppe Garibaldi (not shown), the general who led Italy's troops to the unification of Italy in the 1870s. Garibaldi's men are also honored with statues throughout the park.

The **Fontana di Trevi (pp. 22-23)**, or Trevi Fountain, was finished in 1762, but is the endpoint of an aqueduct that dates all the way back to 19 BC, bringing fresh water to Rome from miles and miles away. At the fountain's center stands a statue of Ocean, who represents an immense river, the source of all the water on earth. Statues of triton are part of the fountain too. One of the tritons is blowing his conch shell, controlling the waves and water. Another bit of mythology around the Trevi Fountain is this: if you turn your back to the fountain and throw a coin into it with your right hand over your left shoulder, you will be sure to return to Rome!

One of the biggest rivers in all of Italy, the **Tiber (pp. 24-25)** runs through Rome, and has always been important to the city. The legend of Romulus and Remus tells the story of the twin brothers being abandoned on the waters of the Tiber before being rescued by a she-wolf, *Lupa*. One of these twins, Romulus, grew up to found the city of Rome. The image of *Lupa* feeding the twins remains the symbol of Rome – and its soccer team – to this day!

The **Keats-Shelley house (p. 27)** is located right next to the famous **Spanish Steps (p. 26)** in the *Piazza di Spagna*. Rome has long attracted painters, writers, and poets from other places, and this *piazza* is the place where many of them would gather. Rome also has inspired hometown poets of her own, including the famous Trilussa, who wrote in the style and language of everyday, working class people in the city he loved. In the spring the Spanish Steps are filled with flowers, an annual tradition that everyone loves, Romans and visitors alike.

The **Villa Borghese (pp. 28-29)** has one of the most beautiful parks in Rome. It is the perfect place to take a stroll and look out over all the rooftops and domes while contemplating a day spent in one of the world's oldest cities.

CPSIA information can be obtained at www.ICGtesting.com
Printed in the USA
BVIW12n2257180418
513668BV00001B/8